CH00600901

GREAT WAR LITERATURE

A-LEVEL STUDY GUIDE

Written by W Lawrance

on

REGENERATION

Great War Literature A-Level Study Guide on Regeneration
Written by W Lawrance

Published by:
Great War Literature Publishing LLP
Darrington Lodge, Springfield Road, Camberley, Surrey GU15 1AB Great Britain
Web site: www.greatwarliterature.co.uk
E-Mail: editor@greatwarliterature.co.uk

Produced in Great Britain

Published October 2006. Copyright © Wendy Lawrance 2006.
The moral right of the author has been asserted.

ISBN 978-1905378395 (1905378394) Paperback Revised Edition - October 2006

10 9 8 7 6 5 4 3 2 1

First published as e-Book 2004
First published in Paperback 2005

All rights reserved: no part of this publication may be reproduced, stored in a retrieval
system, or transmitted in any form or by any means, electronic, mechanical, photocopying or
otherwise, without the prior written consent of Great War Literature Publishing LLP.

Great War Literature Publishing LLP reserve the right to amend this document without any
prior notification.

This study guide is sold subject to the condition that it shall not, by way of trade or
otherwise, be lent, re-sold, hired out or otherwise circulated without the publisher's prior
consent in any form of binding or cover other than that in which it is published and without
similar conditions being imposed on the subsequent purchaser.

Design and production by Great War Literature Publishing LLP
Typeset in Gill Sans and Trajan Pro

This publication replaces ISBN 978-1905378227 (190537822X).

Great War Literature A-Level Study Guide on

Regeneration

CONTENTS

PREFACE

Great War Literature Study Guides' primary purpose is to provide in-depth analysis of First World War literature for GCSE and A-Level students.

There are plenty of other study guides available and while these make every effort to help with the analysis of war literature, they do so from a more general overview perspective.

Great War Literature Publishing have taken the positive decision to produce a more detailed and in-depth interpretation of selected works for students. We also actively promote the publication of our works in an electronic format via the Internet to give the broadest possible access.

Our publications can be used in isolation or in collaboration with other study guides. It is our aim to provide assistance with your understanding of First World War literature, not to provide the answers to specific questions. This approach provides the resources that allow the student the freedom to reach their own conclusions and express an independent viewpoint.

Great War Literature Study Guides can include elements such as biographical detail, historical significance, character assessment, synopsis of text, and analysis of poetry and themes.

The structure of Great War Literature Study Guides allows the reader to delve into a required section easily without the need to read from beginning to end. This is especially true of our e-Books.

The Great War Literature Study Guides have been thoroughly researched and are the result of over 25 years of experience of studying this particular genre.

Studying literature is not about being right or wrong, it is entirely a matter of opinion. The secret to success is developing the ability to form these opinions and to deliver them succinctly and reinforce them with quotes and clear references from the text.

Great War Literature Study Guides help to extend your knowledge of First World War literature and offer clear definitions and guidance to enhance your studying. Our clear and simple layouts make the guides easy to access and understand.

REGENERATION
A NOVEL BY PAT BARKER

INTRODUCTION

Regeneration is, as its title implies, a novel about the rebuilding of men following extreme trauma. The story includes many factual circumstances, using the real names of the people involved. Of the main characters at Craiglockhart, only Billy Prior is fictional. Siegfried Sassoon, Wilfred Owen, Robert Graves and Dr Rivers and his colleagues were all real people and many of the circumstances in which they find themselves, really happened. This mixture of fact and fiction has allowed Pat Barker to inject an air of realism into the story which may otherwise have proved difficult.

The inclusion of the real characters, who are of necessity, more rounded and realistic, enables the reader to more easily accept the fictitious ones. To further this realism, Pat Barker has also used excerpts from Siegfried Sassoons' poems, either directly or in paraphrase, within the text. These examples can be seen in chapters one and fourteen where there are references to *Attack* and *Banishment*. Both of these poems were written while Sassoon was at Craiglockhart.

The author also uses entire poems to great effect. These tell us, very quickly, about Sassoon's state of mind and by River's reaction we learn more about *his* character and the growing relationship between poet and doctor. These poetic references are also used to reinforce the historic and factual elements of the book.

The officers we meet are, with one exception, upper or middle class. The exception is, of course, Billy Prior who, as the perceived hero of the story, has to overcome his disadvantaged youth and unseemly parents. Prior has also been given a difficult and in many ways unattractive personality - he is flippant, sarcastic and coarse. The reader must see through these traits, as Rivers does, to find the real person underneath.

Prior's sexual attitudes and activities are brought into the story to juxtapose those of Siegfried Sassoon, who we are led to believe, because of his status and reputation, has more to lose in the exposure of his sexual 'secret' and must, therefore, unlike Prior, learn to control his urges.

Regeneration is a story of man's exploration of his inner being - his mind, feelings and reactions. It details the effects of war on a generation of young men who, because of their experiences, would never again be able to live ordinary lives.

SYNOPSIS

Chapter One

This begins with Siegfried Sassoon's famous Statement. Dr Rivers is informed that Sassoon is being sent to Craiglockhart. He wonders if the real reason for this is Sassoon's Statement, rather than genuine neurasthenia - is it convenient for the authorities to have him declared neurotic rather than admit there could be any accuracy in his stated opinion?

Sassoon, while on the train bound for Edinburgh, recalls his last meeting with his friend and fellow poet, Robert Graves, when Graves swore that accepting the Medical Board and its consequences was Sassoon's best hope of salvation as the authorities would never court-martial him. Graves, however, being notoriously unreliable, has missed the train, so Sassoon must travel to Craiglockhart alone.

Meanwhile, Rivers reflects on Sassoon's stance and wonders about the poet's state of mind, concluding that he may find himself in a difficult position if he is duty bound to treat a man who is not actually unwell, but simply does not want to continue fighting for whatever reason. He recalls a similar case in the past, and the heated discussions which this had provoked between the doctors. He witnesses Sassoon's nervous arrival at the hospital.

Chapter Two

Sassoon and Rivers meet over tea and discuss Sassoon's recent Medical Board examination which resulted in him being sent to Craiglockhart. It is the opinion of Sassoon that the Board was manipulated by Graves, who saw it as imperative that Sassoon be declared a neurasthenic, rather than be court-martialled. Rivers is initially reluctant to accept this theory and they discuss Sassoon's symptoms which include nightmares and hallucinations. Rivers admits that he doesn't believe that Sassoon is neurotic at all, but states his intention of 'treating' Sassoon.

Later, Rivers discusses his findings with Bryce (Commanding Officer of Craiglockhart). During dinner Sassoon meets a man named Anderson, who seems keen that they should play golf together. A man, named Burns, is violently sick during the meal. We later discover that Burns is deeply traumatised by the experience of being thrown into the air by an explosion and, upon landing, finding himself face-down in the stomach of a decomposing corpse. He is now unable to eat and vomits almost continuously. This case clearly troubles Rivers.

Somewhat belatedly, Robert Graves arrives.

Chapter Three

Rivers and Graves talk and Graves admits that he lied to Sassoon about the court-martial. If Sassoon had continued with his controversial action, the authorities might well have been forced to act against him. Both Graves and Rivers feel that, in the circumstances, Graves did the best thing he could for Sassoon.

Sassoon gives Rivers some of his poems to read which makes Rivers realise that his task of counselling Sassoon to retract his statement and return to the front is going to be more difficult than he had thought: Sassoon didn't write his Statement in a moment of irresponsible madness... his poetry shows that he believes with utter conviction that the *war* is mad.

Chapter Four

Rivers has a discussion with a patient named Anderson - a surgeon who had been serving with the Royal Army Medical Corps, but has suffered a breakdown and despite family responsibilities, is unwilling to return to medicine. Rivers worries that Anderson may be suicidal. The following day, Sassoon and Rivers discuss Sassoon's childhood, education and his life before the war. Sassoon says he believes that the Army is in all probability the only place he has ever felt at home. Rivers, seeming to believe that he may have found a way of treating Sassoon, points out that if he continues with his protest, he'll spend the rest of the war isolated in Craiglockhart, while others are dying. Sassoon replies angrily that if the majority of the population can tolerate such a situation, why shouldn't he?

Burns leaves the hospital, and goes for a walk in the country, eventually returning in the late afternoon. He'd been frightened and disturbed but eventually happy outside of the hospital - more at peace. Once he returns, he realises how much he needs help from Dr. Rivers.

Chapter Five

At Sister Rogers' request, Rivers meets Billy Prior - a young Second Lieutenant who refuses to talk and will only communicate by writing down what he wants to say. He appears angry and dismissive, unwilling to be helped or to help himself.

Graves returns to Liverpool. Once he has said goodbye to his friend, Sassoon returns to Craiglockhart, analysing his own feelings about his safety compared to that of others.

Rivers has a disturbing dream which he struggles to analyse although its roots are based in fact - an experiment in nerve regeneration in which he had participated before the war. On a deeper level, he believes that his treatment of his patients is working, but in some cases - particularly that of Burns - he feels the treatment may, in itself, be cruel. Forcing someone to remember and discuss an abhorrent experience may not be justified in every case.

Chapter Six

Billy Prior has started talking. Rivers tries to get him to talk about his experiences in the trenches. Eventually, Prior tells Rivers of a time when he spent two days standing in a water-filled dug-out, being shelled. Whilst this episode caused him to be taken to a Casualty Clearing Station with abnormal reflexes, it is not the reason he is in Craiglockhart. Prior won't talk about that yet. Later that day, Prior's parents visit. Prior won't talk to his father - he claims his mutism has returned. Rivers, on speaking with Mr Prior has the impression that he looks upon his son with nothing but contempt. Mrs Prior, on the other hand, is much more sympathetic and quite over-protective towards Billy. Prior's asthma, which had been a problem in his childhood, but of which Rivers was unaware, is triggered by this visit. He is moved to the sick bay but worries that he will have to be moved to another hospital. He protests that he is concerned because he has grown accustomed to Craiglockhart and does not want to change situation again, but the inference is that he now trusts Rivers - he just won't admit it yet.

Chapter Seven

Sassoon wakes in the early hours of the morning to the sound of screams and footsteps. He remembers that, by now, his Statement will have been read in the House of Commons and wonders what will happen next.

Rivers visits Prior - it was he who had been screaming during the night. Prior won't discuss his nightmare but says that he will accept hypnotism as a form of treatment. Rivers tells him that this will be done only as a last resort.

A report appears in *The Times* about Sassoon's Statement, pointing out that this brave officer should be an object of sympathy due to his nervous condition. Sassoon is disappointed by this reaction. Rivers persuades him that this is hardly unexpected and suggests that as well as seeing him three times a week, Sassoon should try and make friends and take more exercise. Rivers also suggests that he will nominate Sassoon as a member of the Conservative Club so he can have somewhere to concentrate on his writing.

During the Medical Officer's case conference, Rivers explains to Dr Brock (a colleague) how he views Sassoon's case: it is Sassoon's duty to go back to France and it is River's duty to ensure that he does. Brock, perceptively, realises that this may cause Rivers a great deal of personal torment.

Chapter Eight

Rivers and Prior have another discussion. Prior remembers a time at the front when, during an attack, he ended up in a crater with several other men. Most survived and got back to their own lines, but they weren't relieved and had to stay in the front line. His tone during this conversation is flippant.

Sassoon meets a young officer, named Wilfred Owen. Owen brings five copies of *The Old Huntsman* [Sassoon's most recent volume of poetry] to Sassoon's room, asking him to sign them. They talk for a short while about the war, pacifism and poetry. Sassoon asks Owen to show him some of his poems.

Sassoon and Anderson play golf. Anderson behaves badly when he thinks he is going to lose the game - rather like a small boy who has failed to get his own way. Afterwards, they discuss golf - they never discuss the war, but we learn that Anderson thinks Sassoon's Statement was self-important.

Billy Prior goes to Edinburgh for the evening and meets Sarah Lumb, a factory worker. After several drinks, she tells him how her boyfriend died at Loos and how she came to be working in a munitions factory. On the way home, Billy tries to have sex with her, but she refuses, and they arrange to meet the following Sunday. Billy is so late getting back to Craiglockhart that the doors are locked.

Chapter Nine

Prior is restricted to the hospital for two weeks as a punishment for staying out late. Rivers and Prior discuss River's stammer and how neurasthenia manifests itself in different ways. That evening Prior apologises to Rivers for his behaviour - he had been quite rude - although as Rivers points out, not nearly as rude as he *could* have been. Rivers realises that Prior is becoming depressed so he offers to hypnotise him to see if they can discover whatever it is that Prior can't remember.

During the hypnosis, Prior remembers waking up in a dugout, going out into the trench at stand-to; exchanging a few words with two of his men - Sawdon and Towers and then passing along the trench. A shell hits the trench and when Prior returns, he finds there is almost nothing left of Sawdon and Towers. He and another man, Logan, are clearing up the mess when Prior notices an eyeball between the duckboards. He picks it up and from that moment he is unable to talk. Logan takes him back to the Casualty Clearing Station, but by now Prior can't even remember why he is there.

When the hypnosis is over, Prior is upset and angry. He assumed the reason for his breakdown would have been more traumatic. He had remembered that two of his men had been killed, but had assumed that it must have somehow been his fault and that that was the reason he couldn't remember. He feels ashamed to have broken down over something which seems to him mundane and trivial. Rivers explains that breakdowns can occur by a process of being worn down to a point where continuation with normal life becomes impossible.

Later that night, Rivers realises how tired he is, both physically and mentally. Prior has managed to get under his skin - to see inside him - and that makes Rivers feel uncomfortable.

Chapter Ten

Sarah tells her friends that Billy didn't arrive for their date and while she pretends she doesn't care, it is clear that she is really disappointed.

Rivers attends to a patient named Willard, who despite having no physical injury, cannot walk. Rivers refutes Willard's claim that he must be a coward who cannot face going back - after all a coward would require the use of his legs, even if only to run away.

Rivers and Sassoon meet for lunch at the Conservative Club. Rivers realises that he feels aggrieved at Sassoon's innate capacity to make him question his own views about the war. Sassoon is starting to doubt whether he can continue with his protest when his friends are being killed and wounded. Rivers knows that he can persuade Sassoon to go back, but he has too much respect for Sassoon to manipulate him.

Chapter Eleven

Owen and Sassoon meet again. Sassoon tells Owen that he has realised Rivers will probably succeed in wearing down his protests. Sassoon offers to help Owen with his poetry.

Chapter Twelve

Prior goes to meet Sarah, who, when he explains the circumstances, agrees to forgive him for letting her down the previous weekend. They decide to get away from Edinburgh and go the seaside. Initially Prior feels hostile towards Sarah - he thinks she's like all the other people around him - safe and oblivious to the war - but soon his hostility wanes. There is a thunderstorm and they take shelter in some bushes where they make love. Afterwards, Billy's attitude to Sarah hardens again. He doesn't want to admit to himself that he cares about her.

Chapter Thirteen

Burns appears before the Medical Board where Rivers recommends an unconditional discharge. Prior is back in the sick bay. It would seem that on his way back from the beach, he fainted in the train and Sarah had to help him get back. Rivers is concerned about Prior's asthma, but Prior is adamant that he's well enough to return to France.

Anderson experiences an extreme reaction when his room-mate cuts himself shaving. This worrying aversion to blood makes Rivers realise that Anderson is unlikely to be able to return to medicine and yet he cannot remain at Craiglockhart indefinitely. Rivers is feeling exceptionally tired and ill and believes he must himself be suffering from a war neurosis. Bryce examines him and orders him to take three weeks leave.

Later that evening Sassoon visits Owen and they work on one of Owen's poems [which will become *Anthem for Doomed Youth*]. Afterwards, Sassoon thinks about his men out in France and wonders how many of them are still alive. During the night, he wakes and sees one of his men, Orme, standing in the doorway. However, he knows that Orme is dead. Next day, he goes early to see Rivers, hoping to be able to discuss his hallucination before Rivers leaves; but he's too late - Rivers has already gone. Sassoon feels desolate and abandoned, realising and accepting that Rivers has become a father-figure to him.

Chapter Fourteen

Rivers is staying with his brother Charles. He reminisces about his childhood, remembering his speech therapy sessions with his father; the forming of his own opinions and how they were completely at odds with those of his father. Opening the window, he can hear the thudding of the guns and decides he must write to Sassoon.

Back at Craiglockhart, Sassoon and Owen meet again. Owen has finished his poem and Sassoon is impressed, offering to help him get it published.

Sarah goes to a convalescent hospital with her friend Madge to visit Madge's fiancé who has been wounded. Luckily, his wounds are not severe, so Sarah leaves the couple and decides to wait outside for her friend. She gets lost trying to find her way out of the hospital and stumbles upon a room full of amputees. She is shocked, both by what she sees and by the fact that these men seem to be hidden away, as though they are something to be ashamed of.

She unexpectedly meets Billy, who is also visiting the hospital for a chest examination. They agree to spend some time together. This time, Billy is unreservedly pleased to see Sarah - he even buys her some flowers.

Rivers is now staying with Henry and Ruth Head in London. Henry tells Rivers that there is a job vacancy at the Royal Flying Corps hospital, which would suit Rivers perfectly if he is interested in getting away from Craiglockhart. Rivers feels too much loyalty to Bryce to accept immediately, but tells Henry that he will consider the offer.

Chapter Fifteen

Rivers travels to Suffolk to spend some time with Burns, who is now discharged from Craiglockhart. It soon becomes clear that Burns is still deeply troubled. He continues to have nightmares and cannot face mealtimes. While on a walk with Rivers, Burns comes across a pile of fish-heads and this sight causes a relapse in his physical condition.

One night, there is a terrible storm and the lifeboat is summoned. Rivers is unable to find Burns in the house and goes out looking for him, finding him eventually, cowering in the moat of an old Tower. Rivers manages to lead him back to safety, while being aware that Burns, by now shaking and disoriented, desperately needs help. The next day, Burns finally talks for the first time, about some of his experiences in France. Rivers sees that there is a ray of hope for this young man; he might one day be able to recover.

Chapter Sixteen

Rivers returns to Craiglockhart, his mind almost decided to accept the RFC job offer. He feels more reconciled to his work now. He has a conversation with Sassoon, during which Sassoon reveals his hallucinations of dead friends. He says these images always have puzzled faces, because, he assumes, they cannot understand why he is at Craiglockhart rather than at the front. He has written a poem [Sick Leave], which he asks Rivers to read. Rivers is deeply moved by this poem and Sassoon tells him that he's decided to go back to France.

Chapter Seventeen

Sarah's mother, Ada, visits Edinburgh. Sarah tells her about Billy and says that if he is released from the hospital soon, they will visit Ada while he is on leave.

Graves visits Sassoon. They discuss Owen and his poetry and Sassoon tells Graves of his decision to go back to France. Graves tells Sassoon that a school friend of his has been arrested for soliciting and will soon be sent to Rivers, who will, of course, effect a cure for this deviant behaviour. He points out that he has become friends with Nancy Nicholson and is keen to inform Sassoon that he is not a homosexual.

Sarah and her friends discuss Betty, one of Sarah's friends, who after a failed attempt to abort her pregnancy, is now in hospital.

On the night before Sassoon is due to attend the Medical Board, he and Rivers talk about his chances of getting the decision he wants: to go back to his men in France. Sassoon also tells Rivers about Graves' homosexual friend. They discuss Sassoon's sexuality and the public attitude to homosexuality, particularly in war time. Rivers points out to Sassoon that he should try to conform more and behave in an acceptable manner in all aspects of his life, or risk damaging himself, and his reputation.

Chapter Eighteen

It is the day of the Medical Board. Prior is tense during his questioning, and doesn't help his case with abrupt responses. Sassoon grows impatient, waiting for his appointment, and eventually storms out of the waiting room. Prior is awarded permanent home service and is very unhappy, having hoped to return to France. Rivers explains to him that physically he will never be well enough to return to active service. Prior reveals that his disappointment is due to the fact that now he cannot prove his courage - to himself. He asks Rivers if he may write to him in the future, and Rivers gladly agrees.

By dinner time it has become clear that Sassoon has deliberately avoided his Medical Board. When he does return, Rivers is angry with him. Sassoon admits that he could not bring himself to go before the Board - he was worried that if he went back to the front and still found it necessary to continue his protest, the authorities would say he'd had a relapse and send him back to Craiglockhart. He had contemplated seeking a second opinion as to his sanity in order to make an implied relapse impossible. Rivers is confused by this, thinking that Sassoon means to continue his protest and not return to the front. Sassoon refutes this suggestion - he will definitely go back.

Chapter Nineteen

Prior, now on leave, sneaks into Sarah's lodgings one night. This is their first opportunity to be together without being rushed. While laying on her bed, Prior realises that he can never tell Sarah everything - about his experiences in France and their effects - because he needs to have someone in his life who doesn't know his secrets. He also realises, and tells her, that he loves her. Sarah is pleased - she loves him too.

Sassoon and Owen dine at the Conservative Club. Owen is to leave Craiglockhart. Sassoon is still awaiting news of his posting from the war office. Sassoon dreads the thought of remaining at Craiglockhart without Owen and Rivers, who has also announced his own imminent departure for London. After Sassoon has left, Owen finds the loss of Sassoon's company and friendship difficult to contemplate.

Chapter Twenty

Rivers is about to leave. On his last evening he goes to see Sassoon, who has been visited that day by Lady Ottoline Morrell - a pacifist friend. They talk briefly and Rivers is struck by Sassoon's defeatism and his own role in Sassoon's current predicament: Rivers feels guilty at his involvement in the failure of Sassoon's Declaration. He promises to return for Sassoon's Medical Board.

Soon after his arrival in London, Rivers accepts an invitation to visit Dr Yealland at the National Hospital. Yealland shows Rivers around various wards and describes some of the treatments he will carry out. These include electric shock treatment. His methods are at odds with those advocated and practiced by Rivers.

Chapter Twenty-One

Rivers witnesses Yealland's treatment of a man named Callan, who has been unable to talk since having a breakdown several months earlier. The treatment consists of electric shocks on the back of the throat and outside of the neck. Callan is kept locked in the room with Yealland until he speaks. When this cure has been exacted, Yealland declares that he finds Callan's smile quite offensive and carries out further electrode treatment until Callan doesn't smile any more.

Chapter Twenty-Two

On returning home, Rivers is disturbed by what he has witnessed and his subsequent confrontation with Yealland and is unable to sleep. He decides he must be unwell and resolves to go for a walk on Hampstead Heath. He is still haunted by the day's events, but eventually returns home, feeling physically better. Once asleep, he dreams. His dream is a mixture of the days' experiences and Sassoon's words formed into a nightmarish scenario and he wakes, crying out. He attempts to decipher the meaning of his dream, his conclusion being that, in persuading Sassoon to return to the front, he has silenced his protest and robbed Sassoon of his quite justified and completely sane opinions.

Chapter Twenty-Three

The following morning, Rivers discusses this feeling with Henry Head who points out that, being an honourable man, Sassoon would have gone back to his men anyway, especially once it became clear that his protest wasn't working. Head also reassures Rivers that Yealland's methods and his own are poles apart. Rivers is worried that Sassoon is going back to the front because he wants to die.

Rivers returns to Craiglockhart and has a worrying interview with Anderson who must soon decide what to do - he is unable to return to medicine, but what else is there for him?

Sassoon and Rivers talk about Owen who has been writing excessively emotional letters to Sassoon. Owen had always hero-worshipped Sassoon, but now Sassoon fears that Owen's feelings may have run a little deeper than he had realised.

The following day, the Medical Board sits. When Sassoon's case is reached, Rivers recommends him for general service overseas - an unusual stance given that most Craiglockhart patients are never initially discharged in this manner, but tend to be recommended for home service instead. During his interview, Sassoon makes it very clear that he has not abandoned his protest, but, with prompting from Rivers, confirms that he wants to return to the front.

Sassoon and Rivers bid one another farewell - there is a mutual respect and genuine affection between the two men. Once alone, Rivers realises how meeting Sassoon has changed his own personality and his outlook both towards his work and the war itself. He worries that Sassoon's intentions in going back to France are suicidal - not merely his professed worries about his men. Rivers knows that, whatever the outcome, encouraging Sassoon to go back to France, was his only chance - to remain safely at home would have meant a more certain death than anything that could happen to him in the war.

CHARACTERS

In this section we have concentrated on the characters of Billy Prior and Sarah Lumb only, as they are the main fictional characters involved in *Regeneration*. In addition, there is a section on the author's use of characters in general, both real and fictional, within the novel. Biographies of Siegfried Sassoon, Wilfred Owen and Dr W H R Rivers can be found in the following chapter.

BILLY PRIOR

Prior is a 22 year old Second Lieutenant whose neurosis manifests itself, initially, through an inability to talk or remember the events which have led to his breakdown.

His background is working-class, but his over-protective, ambitious mother has always done her best to push her son up the social ladder, regardless of whether this is best for him. This has led to some confusion on Prior's part as he does not really feel that he belongs anywhere. He is no more at home with upper-class officers, or working-class ranking soldiers, so he effectively drifts in his own personal No Man's Land. In addition, Mrs Prior's desire for her son to 'better himself' has created a rebellious tendency in Billy, who continually questions authority.

He is an intelligent and inquisitive man, unprepared to accept the stereotypes which are thrust upon him - except for one: he believes that because he broke down, his courage *must* have failed him. The fact that he cannot remember the events which led up to his breakdown reinforces this attitude and makes him feel that he must have done something wrong - something so terrible that his only form of self-defence is to forget that it even happened. He is quite shocked to learn that his neurosis is the result of an event which he considers insignificant and commonplace - no worse in fact than any of the other sickening things which have occurred during his time in France. His reaction to this discovery is an angry and emotional outburst which demonstrates how raw his feelings are.

His initial response to his problems, once his voice has returned, is to be defensive - not physically but verbally: he invariably answers a question by asking another question himself. He is reluctant to reveal his feelings or acknowledge the truth. However, he is embarrassed by his lack of control. His nightmares and the consequences of his nocturnal outbursts cause him to feel ashamed of himself. His desire to impress Rivers is interesting - it would seem that he has never really been interested in impressing anyone else. This shows that he is developing a deeper respect for Rivers than even he is prepared to admit.

Prior has a flippant, cynical attitude and his discussions with Rivers are frequently tinged with sarcasm both against Rivers and his methods, and against the war in general. His outlook is nearly always negative which reflects his feelings towards others, but also allows him to hide behind a mask of indifference. His descriptions of his time in France show that he had been capable of caring for others and sympathising with their troubles, but he does not wish to lower his guard and let Rivers, or anyone else, see that he feels anything at all - to Prior that would be a sign of weakness.

Prior's mental turmoil stems from several factors including his upbringing and his war experiences but this is exacerbated by his confusion over sex. He describes his feelings at going into battle in sexual terms; his war-time nightmares and sexual dreams become confused and this brings on a sense of self-revulsion. This, in turn, leads Prior further into depression as he finds it almost impossible to reconcile these two sides of his own personality. Prior's sexual frustrations are bound up with his war neurosis and his need to prove himself - both as a soldier and a man. This is entirely self-inflicted since no-one else seems to doubt him. One could also question whether Prior's attitude to sex shows that he has initially tried to isolate all of his emotions. He is detached from everything, including himself, so sex becomes a purely physical, rather than emotional, requirement. Eventually, as he begins to come to terms with his war experiences and understand his own need for help, he also becomes more tolerant of and attached to others, including both Rivers and Sarah.

His upbringing and class also have a deep impact on his feelings and reactions. When Rivers tells him that officers tend to suffer with stammering rather than mutism, Prior delves deeply into this statement, pressing Rivers to reveal more about himself than he wishes. This prevents Prior having to face up to his own problems, but also reveals his deep confusion over his own status: his upbringing was working class, so he seems to question whether he should react like a ranking soldier. However, there is no escaping the fact that he is an officer. Does he even know how officers are supposed to react? He appears to have little time for 'upper-class' officers and refuses to accept being associated with them. His shame at breaking down also reflects his bewilderment over his status: men don't break down; they get shot, or blown up, but they don't break down.

He has a deep desire to return to the front and prove to himself that he is not a coward. However, this feeling is restrained - at least in part - by a natural leaning towards self-preservation. This also adds to the confusion in his mind and when he is finally awarded permanent home service, he is left with a sense of self-doubt and a defeatist attitude. He is also ashamed to admit that he feels relieved that he will not have to go back to France and eventually even grudgingly admits to feeling grateful to Rivers for helping him.

Prior is a complex and confused character, who is lost and desperately in need of help. It is only when he is finally prepared to admit this to himself that his road to recovery can begin. Whether it will ever be complete is not clear at the end of this novel.

SARAH LUMB

Sarah is a young woman who works in a factory making detonators. She is living in lodgings away from her family home and is independent and self-reliant. Her job is hard manual work, but she does it for the money and because it means she doesn't have to be subservient to others, as she was in her job as a servant before the war. Sarah represents the new face of women during the war, who had to take on the roles of the absent men.

Sarah is defensive, particularly of her class, and gets angry with Billy over his adoption of superior 'officer' ways - such as censoring his mens' letters. This is a simplistic, inexperienced and, one could argue, uneducated view point: as an officer, Billy has no choice but to censor these letters; he has had to adopt these officer-like qualities, which Sarah finds distasteful, in order to fit in with those around him. Sarah perceives this as a betrayal of his background. While she may not like to accept it, a reality of the war was that officers from the lower classes tended to be ostracised by their upper class equivalents. Billy is also angry about this but reluctantly accepts the situation, being as there is nothing he can do about it.

Sarah is deeply affected by seeing maimed men at the hospital she visits. It is not their injuries which disturb her so much as the fact that these men, who have given so much, are kept out of sight. She also feels guilty that, in bursting into their room, she has made them feel worse - by reminding them of everything they have lost. She has a profound sense of the injustice of their situation, feeling that a *grateful* nation would acknowledge their sacrifices rather than shutting them away. When she tells Billy about this, he begins to see her in a new light - he finds it refreshing that she does not share the callous opinions of so many others with whom he has come into contact.

Sarah has a masculine attitude to life: from her boyish handshake to her reactions to work, the war and those around her. She demonstrates this attitude, also, in her relationship with Billy. She hides her feelings - a more masculine than feminine trait and, while making it clear that she is not entirely averse to having sex with him, this will take place when *she's* ready and not before. She is able to take control of their relationship in a way she would not have been able to before the war. It must be remembered that before the First World War, women did not have the same rights as they did afterwards. Even Billy notices that women seem to have changed. In having to assume traditionally male roles - both at work and in the home - women became more independent. For Sarah, this feeling is enhanced by not having had a father-figure during her childhood and the fact that her mother has a strong character in her own right.

Sarah, like Billy, has a slightly ambiguous character. She can be demure - for example, when she and Billy visit the beach, she is shy about removing her stockings in front of him. Then, within a few minutes, she and Billy are making love in some bushes. Equally, she can be raucous when she is with her friends. This ambiguity further goes to demonstrate the changing role and character of women, whose position in society had itself become confused. They were expected to take the place of men in many ways, but to still retain their feminine qualities.

Sarah is angry about the war - the waste and futility. The death of her boyfriend at Loos has left her incensed that he was killed not by the Germans but by a *British* gas attack. She lacks the complacency generally exhibited by civilians, and never seeks to glorify the sacrifices of those who have died. Therefore, she is not typical of those left at home and this is one of the reasons that Billy is attracted to her.

THE AUTHOR'S USE OF CHARACTERS

Regeneration contains a mixture of real and fictitious characters. The representation of the real characters is, generally speaking, fairly accurate, allowing for "artistic license" in imagined conversations and personality traits. The use of sometimes stereotypical characters in the novel has the effect of making the real people involved seem somehow more genuine and realistic. For example, the character of Major Huntley, with his passion for roses and opinions on the "racial degeneration" of society represents the callous face of the officer-class. This representation makes the character of Rivers, for example, seem more sensible and sympathetic.

Similarly, the episode concerning Dr. Yealland's treatment of Callan opposes Rivers's treatment of Billy Prior. Both Prior and Callan exhibit similar symptoms, yet the two doctors treat their patients in completely different ways. Once again, the reader becomes more appreciative of Rivers's personality and his methods. We are continually being reminded of the personal cost to Rivers, however, as he himself undergoes a breakdown while Yealland is shown to be unaffected by his patients or their problems.

The character of Billy Prior, as the flawed representative of the lower-class type of officer provides a good contrast with Siegfried Sassoon and, to a lesser extent, Wilfred Owen. Prior, like Owen, harbours doubts about his own bravery and both men have felt a need to return to the front to prove themselves "worthy". The contrasts and similarities between Prior and Sassoon, as represented in the novel, are more marked. Both men hold the same rank, but while Sassoon socialises at the Conservative Club, on the personal invitation of Dr Rivers, Prior frequents Edinburgh's cafés and public houses. Sassoon's conversations with Rivers are well-mannered, while Prior's are invariably antagonistic. This device is used to remind us that these two men, while expected to perform the same duties, have very different backgrounds. Both Sassoon and Prior feel hostile towards the war, but while Sassoon has chosen to act upon his feelings, Prior remains passive - sensing and understanding that such a demonstration would achieve nothing. One could interpret this as the author's means of demonstrating Prior's superior grasp of the situation - even, it could be argued, his greater level of common sense. Sassoon gradually comes to appreciate that his protest has achieved nothing, but this is a fact of which Prior would have always been aware.

The sexuality of these two men is also a strong feature of the novel. Prior is represented as sexually frustrated at the beginning and, even following his "conquest" of Sarah. Until he begins to accept his own feelings, he remains confused about his reactions to her. Sassoon, on the other hand, is portrayed as struggling to come to terms with his sexuality. Sassoon's discussions with Dr Rivers on the subject are used to reveal the close nature of their friendship and the mutual trust which has developed between them. Whenever Prior and Rivers discuss sex, it is done, at least on Prior's side, with an element of cynicism, or even anger, although this could also be interpreted as embarrassment. Prior's sexual frustrations are represented somewhat coarsely, while Sassoon's are shown in a more genteel light. Prior has, at one stage, a callous need for revenge, which he contemplates exacting by making Sarah "pay". This action seems to be well within the realms of possibility for his character, although he does ultimately calm down. On the other hand, when Sassoon is said to be experiencing a sexual anger - at the Conservative Club - this is qualified as being out of character. Once again, these differences in how the characters react to a similar situation reinforce the contrasts in their two personalities as well as making the reader question which of the two is the more sympathetic character.

The women in the novel are also treated in a fairly stereotypical fashion. In order to demonstrate the changing role of women, the author gives many of them masculine traits, but reminds us of their feminine vulnerability at the same time. For example, Sarah's demeanour and language are not always traditionally "feminine", yet when she and Billy have made love for the first time, her reaction is more female. She worries Billy with her closeness, to the point where he finds it necessary to push her away and antagonise her into more "masculine" behaviour.

The relationships between men and women are shown to often be confusing and, in many ways, different from pre-war conceptions of the male/female role. For example, neither Willard or Anderson seem very keen, or ultimately very pleased, to see their wives. Their role within the family has changed, as during their prolonged absence, the women have taken over many of their roles. In addition to their own neurological problems, these men must also confront their altered status within the home, especially as they may no longer be able to fight for their country, or even work to bring money into the household.

BIOGRAPHIES

SIEGFRIED SASSOON

Siegfried Loraine Sassoon was born on 8th September 1886 at the family home, Weirleigh, at Matfield in Kent. He was the middle of three sons of Alfred and Theresa Sassoon. Alfred was from a wealthy Jewish banking family, but had been disowned by his mother upon his marriage to Theresa, who was not of the Jewish faith. Theresa was a Thornycroft by birth, with an intelligent and artistic nature. She was a strong, independent woman and was very protective of her talented son. Alfred and Theresa separated when Siegfried was five years old and Alfred died four years later of tuberculosis. Siegfried passed a happy and secure childhood, enjoying reading, music, nature and, of course, writing poetry. He was educated at Marlborough and then went on to Clare College, Cambridge, where he studied Law and History, but left without obtaining a degree.

Back at home in Kent, he led a contented existence - hunting, riding point-to-point races, playing cricket and he continued to write poetry. In March 1914, Sassoon moved to London but, despite the obvious advantages of being in London's literary circle, he struggled to maintain his new lifestyle on his limited allowance.

Upon the outbreak of war, Sassoon put his financial worries behind him and immediately enlisted as a Trooper in the Sussex Yeomanry. A bad fall while riding, however, left him with a broken arm. When he had recovered from this injury, he transferred to the infantry and was commissioned into the Royal Welch Fusiliers in May 1915.

After training, Siegfried left for France on 24 November 1915 and joined the 1st Battalion at Béthune. It was at this time that he met fellow poet and Royal Welch Fusilier, Robert Graves. By now the war had started to become more personal for Siegfried. His younger brother, Hamo, was mortally wounded at Gallipoli and was buried at sea on 1st November 1915. Then on 18th March 1916, his close friend, Second Lieutenant David Thomas was shot in the throat while out with a wiring party, and died of his wound. David Thomas had been an object of great affection for Sassoon, who was moved to write of him in *The Last Meeting*.

These losses had a profound effect on Sassoon and the war became a personal crusade to avenge these deaths. He took to creeping about in front of the British wire, with reckless enthusiasm and soon earned the nickname "Mad Jack". In June his platoon was involved in a raid on Kiel Trench and his selfless actions in retrieving the dead and wounded from No Man's Land earned him the Military Cross. The citation read:

"For conspicuous gallantry during a raid on the enemy's trenches. He remained for one and a half hours under rifle and bomb fire, collecting and bringing in our wounded. Owing to his courage and determination, all the killed and wounded were brought in".

Sassoon went on to take part in the Battle of the Somme, being recommended for another medal, following a bombing raid. In late July Siegfried became ill with trench fever and was sent home to convalesce. He spent some time with Robert Ross, who had been a close friend of Oscar Wilde. Ross, in turn, introduced Siegfried to Arnold Bennett and H.G. Wells. Sassoon returned to France in February 1917 but after just two days, was forced into hospital suffering from German measles. Upon returning to the front, ten days later, he joined the Second Battalion, Royal Welch Fusilliers and participated in the Second Battle of the Scarpe, where he was wounded in the shoulder.

Whilst convalescing in England, Sassoon wrote his infamous Declaration, under the influence, it must be said, of prominent pacifists, such as John Middleton Murry and Bertrand Russell.

Sassoon's intention in making his Declaration had been to receive a court martial, but this was averted by the intervention of his friends including Robert Graves and Edward Marsh. A medical board (after emotional evidence given by Graves) declared that Sassoon was suffering from shell-shock. Sassoon, who had by now become so disillusioned that he had thrown his medal ribbon into the Mersey river, found himself at Craiglockhart War Hospital, in Edinburgh. The diagnosis of shell-shock was one of convenience for the authorities, desperate to avoid the embarrassment of a courageous and decorated officer, publicly and defiantly opposing the continuation of the war.

During his time at Craiglockhart, Sassoon was treated by Dr W. H. R. Rivers, who came to have a great influence over him and the two men remained close friends until the doctor's untimely death in 1922. Another, more famous, meeting at this time, was with Wilfred Owen, who was a fellow patient at Craiglockhart. Sassoon encouraged Owen, in whom he could perceive a genuine and natural talent for writing poetry. He also continued to write many poems himself.

Sassoon suffered from feelings of extreme guilt at being safe at home, while his men were fighting in France, and eventually he reached the decision to return to France. On 26th November 1917, he was passed fit for general service.

On 13th February 1918, Sassoon sailed from Southampton and, following a long journey, arrived in Palestine. After three months there, however, he was posted back to France. Once settled, Sassoon's foolhardiness re-surfaced and after leading a terrified corporal on a raid into No Man's Land, a euphoric Sassoon stood up in a trench and was shot in the head. He later discovered that he had been shot by one of his own sergeants. This wound, while not fatal, was serious enough to mean the end of Siegfried's war and he was placed on indefinite sick leave and eventually retired from the army on 12 March 1919. In the period immediately following the war, Sassoon met many famous writers, including T.E. Lawrence (Lawrence of Arabia) and Thomas Hardy, with whom he frequently visited. He also, briefly, became literary editor of the Daily Herald and while there received a privately printed volume of poems from Edmund Blunden and through shared interests in poetry and cricket, the two became life-long friends.

Sassoon, in 1928, began writing his autobiographies, initially as a fictionalised account in *Memoirs of a Fox-hunting Man*, *Memoirs of an Infantry Officer* and finally *Sherston's Progress*, which are collectively known as *The Complete Memoirs of George Sherston*. He then published the non-fiction versions, entitled *The Old Century and Seven More Years*, *The Weald of Youth* and *Siegfried's Journey*. This is not to say that he ceased writing poetry, but he felt a need to expunge his memories and experiences of the war.

Sassoon's homosexuality, which had remained unfulfilled and dormant throughout the war, heightened, and he embarked on several romantic liaisons, particularly during his travels into Europe during the 1920's. He tired of the fickle nature of these relationships, however, and on 18th December 1933, he married Hester Gatty, daughter of a prominent barrister and the Chief Justice of Gibraltar. In October 1936 Hester and Siegfried had a son, named George. The marriage was not altogether happy. Hester was keen to share her husband's interests and activities, but Sassoon resented her interference and excluded her. They separated in 1945. In 1957, Sassoon was received into the Roman Catholic Church.

Sassoon lived a quiet existence at his home, Heytesbury House in
Wiltshire, until his death on September 1st 1967. He is buried at St
Andrew's Church in the village of Mells in Somerset.

WILFRED OWEN

Wilfred Edward Salter Owen was born on 18th March 1893 in Plas
Wilmot near Oswestry in Shropshire. Until Wilfred was four, the
family lived in relative comfort in a house belonging to his
grandfather, Edward Shaw - a former mayor of the city. Upon Shaw's
death, however, it was discovered that he was virtually bankrupt and
Wilfred and his family were forced, much to his mother's
disappointment, to move to small lodgings in Birkenhead.

Wilfred had three siblings - brothers Colin and William (known by
his second name - Harold) and a sister Mary. Wilfred was educated
at the Birkenhead Institute and, under his mother's influence,
developed into an earnest and slightly arrogant young man. In 1907
the Owens moved again - this time to Shrewsbury as Wilfred's
father, Tom, had been appointed Assistant Superintendent of the
Joint Railways. Their living conditions improved, especially with the
addition of open countryside, which was now close at hand.
Wilfred's seat of education became the Technical School in
Shrewsbury where he studied hard. He enjoyed literature, having
begun to write his own poems at about the age of ten and was
then, as always, particularly influenced by the works of Keats.

In 1911 he sat the qualifying exam for London University and
passed, but not with honours and, as his parents were unable to
afford the fees, he required a scholarship which was out of the
question. He took a position as lay assistant to the Vicar of
Dunsden in Oxfordshire in return for which he would receive
tuition. He decided to leave Dunsden in February 1913, having

started to doubt his religious convictions and returned to Shrewsbury. He then sat for a scholarship at Reading University, but failed and decided to put an end his ambition of a university education.

The financial position of his family meant that a career as a poet was impossible, so Wilfred decided to travel to France and work there as a teacher of English in the Berlitz School of Languages. This was not a great success and following an illness, he left in July 1914 to take up the position of private tutor to a wealthy family in the Pyrenees. In the autumn, however, he left this job and took up a similar one with another family which lasted until August 1915.

The outbreak of war initially had little effect on Owen, who continued with his life in France. In a letter to his mother from Bordeaux, dated 2nd December 1914, he speaks of his shame at not enlisting, but justifies this with the knowledge that he is perpetuating the English language: an ideal which he finds more important than any other.

By July 1915, he began to show the first signs of a change of mind. He eventually decided to enlist as he felt he could no longer continue to sit on the side-lines while others were fighting. Owen returned to England in September 1915 and enlisted in the Artists' Rifles in October. Following months of training, he was commissioned into the Manchester Regiment in June 1916. Second Lieutenant Wilfred Owen arrived in France in late December 1916, right in the middle of the worst winter of the war.

On 13th March 1917, Owen fell into a cellar and received a concussion which hospitalised him for two weeks. On his return to his battalion at the beginning of April, he found himself involved in heavy fighting near St Quentin. He was blown off his feet by a shell in Savy Wood and spent several days in a shell-hole surrounded by the dismembered remains of a fellow officer. Although physically unhurt, when Owen's Battalion was relieved on 21st April, it was noticed that his behaviour had become abnormal - he was confused in his speech and appeared shaky. He was thought to be suffering from shell-shock and was sent to a Casualty Clearing Station. Eventually he was sent to Craiglockhart War Hospital in Edinburgh, where he would remain for four months.

While at Craiglockhart, Owen met Siegfried Sassoon, a fellow patient, and the two became friends. Sassoon's reputation as a poet and decorated war hero, had preceded him and the shy, stammering Owen was in awe, but plucked up his courage and introduced himself to the older man. After an initially awkward interview, Sassoon agreed to look at some of Owen's work. Whilst these early efforts were by no means brilliant, Sassoon perceived a natural talent hidden in Owens' poems. The more experienced poet encouraged and assisted his young protégé, even to the point where the manuscript of one of Owen's most famous poems, *Anthem for Doomed Youth*, contains nine amendments and several crossings-out in Sassoon's handwriting. Sassoon also took the opportunity to introduce Owen to Robert Graves, and through him Owen also met Robert Ross and H. G. Wells, among many others.

Owen was declared fit for light duties and left Craiglockhart for Scarborough. By the end of August 1918 he was back in France. In October, he was awarded the Military Cross. The citation read:

"He personally manipulated a captured machine gun in an isolated position and inflicted considerable losses on the enemy. Throughout he behaved most gallantly."

On the morning of 4th November, while attempting to cross the Sambre-Oise Canal, Owen was shot and killed. One week later, the Armistice was signed, hostilities ceased and all over England, church bells rang out in celebration. Tom and Susan Owen were listening to these bells and looking forward to the safe return of their beloved eldest son when the telegram arrived announcing his death.

Wilfred Owen is buried in the tiny Commonwealth War Graves Commission cemetery at Ors.

DR W H R RIVERS

William Halse Rivers Rivers was born near Chatham in Kent, on March 12th 1864, the oldest of four children of Henry and Elizabeth Rivers. Henry Rivers was a clergyman, as well as being a speech therapist and farmer. The family home, Knowles Bank at Tonbridge in Kent, was also a place of residence for many pupils from all over the country who went there to be cured of their speech impediments. William himself suffered with a stammer which, while it never completely disappeared, did become less bothersome in his later life.

William was educated in Brighton in West Sussex and then attended a public school close to the family home in Kent. His time here passed smoothly and he showed a keen interest in science. He was due to sit for a scholarship to Cambridge University, but he missed the final year of his schooling and the exam, following a serious bout of typhoid. He chose, instead, to study medicine at the University of London, graduating in 1886.

In 1888 he was elected a Fellow of the Royal College of Physicians and became a resident at St. Bartholomew's Hospital in London the following year. Over the next few years, Rivers travelled and attended lectures, taking a particular interest in psychology. In 1892 he took up a position as Lecturer in Psychological and Experimental Psychology at Cambridge University. Six years later, he took part in an expedition to the Torres Straits to study anthropology. In 1901 he embarked on a longer trip to study in Melanesia.

When he arrived back in Cambridge in 1903 he began working with Henry Head on a study of the regeneration of nerves. This work, which involved the severing of nerves in Head's arm, would take four years to complete.

Rivers was attending a conference in Australia when the First World War was declared and returned to England in the Spring of 1915. He initially worked as a civilian doctor at Mughill Military Hospital in Lancashire, but in 1916 was made a captain in the Royal Army Medical Corps, transferring to Craiglockhart War Hospital that autumn.

Among his many patients at Craiglockhart, was Siegfried Sassoon who was there officially to be treated for shell-shock. Both men knew that Sassoon was not suffering from this condition, but it was Rivers' duty, nonetheless, to persuade Sassoon to go back to the front. He succeeded in this mission, but at considerable cost to himself. His conversations with, and belief in, Sassoon caused Rivers a great deal of conflict between doing what he believed was right, and doing his duty.

Sassoon and Rivers became friends and after the war, when Rivers had returned to Cambridge, he often visited Sassoon at his family home. Sassoon always felt a sense of gratitude to Rivers for his help and also for believing in him at a time when he was beginning to doubt himself. This friendship was cut short by Rivers' untimely death on 4th June 1922, from a strangulated hernia.

THEMES

RELATIONSHIPS

This is one of the fundamental themes of Regeneration, whether it is the relationship between soldiers, parents and children, or men and women.

Billy Prior and Sarah Lumb

Billy and Sarah meet in a café, where she is sitting with a group of friends from the factory where she works. Billy is not instantly attracted to Sarah, initially preferring her friend, Madge. Sarah, however, strikes up a conversation with him and they move on to a hotel for a drink. Due to his embarrassment and need for freedom, Billy has removed his blue badge which denotes his status as a resident at Craiglockhart. During their conversation, Billy learns about Sarah's past, but reveals nothing of himself. In the same way as he is unwilling to share his thoughts with Rivers, he will also not allow Sarah to have any knowledge of him. He is mainly interested in having sex; but he must be in control. When Sarah refuses him, he reluctantly accepts this and kisses her, but makes sure that he is the one to end their embrace. He is telling her, subconsciously, that he is in charge - he has *chosen* not to force her to have sex with him. He feels this way because in every other aspect of his life, he has no control at all and just for once, he wants to dominate a situation. So Sarah now becomes a challenge and Billy decides to see her again.

On their second outing, Sarah tells him that despite his precautions, she has always been aware of his residence at Craiglockhart - and what's more it doesn't bother her one bit. She is prepared to accept him for what he is, rather than what the war has made him. On this occasion they go to the seaside. Billy is still feeling sexually frustrated and the physical presence of Sarah is heightening his desire. This feeling, however, dwindles upon their arrival at the beach, when he is struck by how out-of-place he feels amongst the crowds. He even begins to resent Sarah, feeling that she belongs with the complacent hoards of people instead of with him. A storm suddenly erupts and Billy forgets his sense of injustice as his desires are re-aroused. The couple shelter in some bushes and make love.

Afterwards they initially enjoy their sense of shared secrets, but soon Billy senses that he must not let Sarah past his emotional barriers - he tells himself that what has happened between them means nothing. This is another form of self-preservation - by pretending to himself that nothing matters, he can protect himself from caring for anyone, except himself. Sarah is offended by his reaction, although she does her best to hide this and adopts a harsh attitude which mirrors his.

Their next meeting is unplanned and takes place at the hospital. Billy is having his chest inspected and Sarah is visiting Madge's fiancé. This time, Billy is more impressed. Sarah has just come from seeing a group of maimed soldiers and he admires her reaction to this. Sarah does not talk about glory or noble sacrifices, but demonstrates a concerned and realistic attitude to the men's suffering. Billy respects her honesty. He buys her flowers and kisses her - this is the first sign of tenderness and genuine affection he has displayed towards her. There are no ulterior motives this time, instead it is as though Billy has finally realised that Sarah means something to him.

The next time we meet them is after Billy has been awarded permanent home service. Billy goes to Sarah's lodgings after dark and climbs in through a window. He has realised that he cannot tell Sarah why he had his breakdown: but this is not done to protect her - her ignorance is more comforting to him than her knowledge. He still feels the need to have somewhere to hide from the realities of the war and what he has experienced. If Sarah knew the truth, he might feel obliged to discuss it with her - this way, when he is with her, he can pretend his problems do not exist. He tells Sarah that he loves her and reassures her that he has no ulterior motive in saying this. She is pleased because she loves him too.

Billy's affection for Sarah is slow to develop - initially he sees her only as a means to an end: he needs to have sex, and she can provide it. Within this, though, is a necessity to prove himself: he cannot return to the fighting yet, but there are other ways of showing his masculinity. His opinion of her changes as their relationship develops - not only because he comes to understand her better, but also because of his increasing knowledge of himself. He has to learn to manage his own emotions and eventually becomes more able to deal with those of another person.

Sarah's attraction to Billy is more instant. She refuses to have sex with him on their first date - she wants to see him again and allows him to walk her home so that he will know where she lives. When Billy is unable to keep their second appointment, she is disappointed although she does her best to conceal this from her friends. When Billy does visit, she is angry - her independence shows through - but soon relents on hearing his explanation.

Their meeting at the hospital is a turning point in their relationship. She realises that she's been looking forward to seeing him again and greets him with unconcealed pleasure - showing that she no longer finds it necessary to hide her feelings. The same applies to Billy, who, for the first time, is able to exhibit outward signs of affection for Sarah.

At the point where we leave Billy and Sarah, their future looks promising - he is safe from the war and they both profess to be in love.

Billy Prior and his Parents

Billy has had difficult and contrasting relationships with both of his parents. His mother has always tried to protect him. As a child she kept him indoors, ostensibly because of his asthma, but this also provided the perfect excuse to shield him from the neighbourhood boys who she felt were socially inferior to her son. She has always had high ambitions for him, encouraging him to become a clerk in the shipping office, rather than a manual worker, like his father. She is proud of the fact that he has become an officer.

Mrs Prior knows that Billy does not appreciate her interference, but she fails to understand why: she doesn't realise that she has put him in a position where he feels he doesn't belong. Through her own intense desire for her son to do well, she has stifled his ambitions: he quashes his own idea of entering politics, because he doesn't feel he is sufficiently well educated to succeed. He feels that he would, once again, be like a fish out of water.

Billy's father has a much more down-to-earth, harsh attitude to his son. He had a hard childhood himself and resents his son having things too easy.

During Billy's childhood, Mr Prior allowed another boy to beat him, to teach him to stand up for himself. Mr Prior is quite proud of the fact that when Billy did eventually retaliate, he nearly killed the other boy. Billy had finally done something worthwhile. Now, however, he is contemptuous of what Billy has become in every sense - as a clerk, as an officer and as a man. Billy's father has no time for neuroses and would have more respect for Billy if he had been physically injured.

Billy has no respect for either of his parents. He resents his mother for interfering in his life and blames her for being too ambitious on his behalf. He would have liked to make more decisions for himself and joining the army in the first week of the War enabled him to break free from her influence. There is no affection between Billy and his father, but then his father is not a man likely to show affection. When his parents visit Craiglockhart, Billy chooses to revert to mutism, rather than talk to them and the stress of this visit triggers an asthma attack. His asthma had been worse when he lived at home, showing that his childhood and homelife were more stressful to him than being involved in the fighting at the front.

The relationship between Mr and Mrs Prior would have tainted Billy's view of love and marriage. His father was physically violent and his mother was subserviently ashamed. As a couple, they have no respect for each other, and witnessing all of this would have, naturally, affected Billy's own capacity to admit love into his relationships with women.

Billy Prior and Dr Rivers

Dr Rivers' first introduction to Billy is via Sister Rogers, who, contrary to her normal behaviour, has taken an instant dislike to the young Second Lieutenant. Initially, of course, Prior cannot speak, so his written answers to Dr Rivers' questions are necessarily short, but still sarcastic, awkward and cynical. Even once he has started to use his voice again, there is little variation in his frequently defensive answers. Rivers is gradually able to break through Billy's defences, allowing him to become more open. His method of doing this is to employ some of Billy's own tactics: for example, when Billy won't co-operate by answering his inquiries, rather than patiently pursuing his line of questioning, he simply terminates their discussion. Billy's desperate response demonstrates that he knows that he needs to talk to Rivers in order to understand why his breakdown happened and ultimately make a recovery.

Billy likes Dr Rivers, but as with most of his relationships, he finds it easier to hide behind a façade of animosity than to admit his true feelings. We do see small chinks in Billy's armour though; he becomes distressed, for example, at the prospect of having to be transferred to another hospital when his asthma flares up. He wants to stay with Rivers, whom he has grown to trust.

Billy resents all the questioning that Rivers must carry out. He is arrogant and wants simply to know and understand what has happened to him, be made well again, and return to France. He overcomes his resentment by questioning Rivers in return. His questions are frequently impertinent and delve into Rivers' private life, but this is another trait of Billy's character. He will, naturally, always look for the weak-spot in his opponent.

Rivers is aware that Billy has penetrated his professional persona. This makes him uncomfortable, but he understands that for Billy to continue with his treatment, and ultimately make a full mental recovery, their strange relationship must be allowed to continue.

Rivers comes to like Billy, despite, and sometimes because of, his faults. He feels that, because of his past, Billy needs defending - frequently from himself - and finds himself quite prepared to adopt that role. Eventually, there exists between these two men, a sense of mutual respect and trust.

Siegfried Sassoon and Dr Rivers

This relationship is more complex to describe, since its foundation is reality. The purpose of Rivers in his treatment of Sassoon is to persuade him to retract his Declaration, attend a Medical Board, which would declare him as recovered from his supposed neurosis and allow him to return to the front. The fundamental problem with this is that Rivers does not believe that Sassoon is suffering from neurosis. Rivers understands that Sassoon's actions stem from a deep desire to end the slaughter - and there is nothing mad about that whatsoever. This makes Rivers' task difficult. His first problem is how to cure a man who he doesn't believe is ill; and secondly, if he does effect this cure, how will he be able to live with his conscience, given that the "cure" will most certainly require an element of breaking Sassoon's perfectly sound spirit, and ultimately it could result in the patient's death?

Rivers is impressed by Sassoon, not just the poet, but the man and, indeed, the officer. It becomes clear that Sassoon is a highly respected and courageous commander who loves his men and regards it as his duty to look after them. The respect between these two men is mutual and almost instantaneous and before long Sassoon has placed Rivers in the role of "Father Figure".

Rivers decides that the best approach with Sassoon is to remind him that by continuing with his protest, he will remain safe, but his men will be dying - without him. Initially, Sassoon's response to this emotive reasoning is that he will just have to accept it. After all, his men will go on dying whether he is there or not, so what difference does it make? Sassoon also expresses his anger that he should be forced to care about the fate of his men, while others remain oblivious. Rivers continues with this treatment, until eventually, Sassoon decides to return to France. This decision signifies a personal victory for both men, but, as with the war itself, victory must necessarily be tinged with loss. They will lose one another, of course, but also there is the very real risk, which Rivers has perceived, that Sassoon has decided to return to the front with the sole intention of getting himself killed. The decision, however, is one which, despite this risk, the doctor must endorse - not because it is his duty, but because he has discovered that for Sassoon to remain safe in England while his men were suffering would, in fact, be a worse fate than anything the war could inflict.

During their sessions, they also discuss Sassoon's sexuality, which is something he is struggling to comprehend himself. Rivers makes it clear that he won't use Sassoon's homosexuality to his disadvantage. He also points out that such sexual tendencies bring an element of danger - discovery would bring ruin and, after all Sassoon is in enough trouble with the authorities as it is. This is not something which Sassoon needs to be told: one of the reasons for his ambiguity on this subject is the fear of discovery and the publicity that would follow. He also understands that one of the reasons why Robbie Ross has to keep his opinions to himself, is that his connection with Oscar Wilde has placed him in a precarious position with the authorities.

Rivers' treatment of Sassoon comes at considerable personal cost to the doctor. He is being forced to confront his own opinions about the validity of the conflict and his part in it. His perceived duty is to make these men face their worst fears, then make them well enough to return to the war and his conscience struggles with this concept.

CONTROL

As a theme in the book, control takes many forms. These vary from a need to control others and demonstrate an element of power over them, to a simple need to have some say in ones own actions and future.

Sassoon, for example, tries to take control of the war, at a personal and ultimately futile level. His Declaration is his attempt at influencing the course of the conflict, which, in his view, has lost its direction and sense of purpose. It isn't that he thinks war is always wrong, just that this particular war and the level of slaughter involved, can no longer be justified. Sassoon, naturally, cannot exert that much influence, and his Declaration fails in its intent.

In getting to the point of making the Declaration, others, including Bertrand Russell and Lady Ottoline Morrell, have exerted considerable influence over Sassoon. For *them* to make such a protest, would carry little weight, as they were known pacifists; but this Statement made by a courageous officer and winner of the Military Cross is a different matter altogether. Sassoon has been controlled and manoeuvred into making his Statement and then Robert Graves takes over the controls and "saves" his friend from his longed-for, publicity-laden, court martial by helping to have him declared neurotic and sent to Craiglockhart. Graves believes that he is acting in Sassoon's best interests, which may well be the case. For Sassoon, however, there is no self-control left in his life - he has become a passive observer of events over which he has no influence. Eventually, this unwelcome passivity is one of the elements which drives him back to the conflict, although he dictates that he must be allowed to fight, not be put safely behind a desk. This shows Sassoon regaining control of his life and the direction which he wants it to follow - regardless of the consequences.

Rivers exerts control over his patients, but not in the same manifestly obvious way as Dr Yealland. For Rivers, the way to control the minds of the men he must treat is to force them to remember their horrors and face up to them, thereby diminishing the role of the neurosis to a memory and enabling the patient to regain control of himself. Rivers continually doubts the role which he plays in curing these men, as well as his ability to always succeed. In Burns, for example, Rivers seems to think he has met his match. Nothing which he has tried on this young man has really worked, and although there are some improvements in Burns's state of mind, his future is bleak. Rivers harbours concerns that to even attempt to control a man's mind in this way is counter-productive: especially if the result is the man's death once he has returned to the fighting.

Dr Yealland's methods, as portrayed, are less subtle. His control is more absolute and he is much less forgiving of failure. The portrayal of Yealland shows us that Rivers's methods, despite his own misgivings, are kinder and more humane.

Billy Prior tries to exert control over everyone he comes across. In his relationship with Sarah, he feels it is he that should dominate: he must be the one to decide when they make love, and where. He wants to dictate the pace of their relationship - in fact at the beginning he is unwilling to admit they even have a relationship. In his conversations with Rivers, Prior is always trying to take control of the situation, by asking, rather than answering, questions. He shows little concern at the time for how Rivers may feel about his questioning, he just knows that he cannot stand being subservient.

Billy's need to control as many aspects of his life a possible stems partly from his childhood and also from his war experiences. His mother's dominance of his early life and her decisions as to how he should behave have left him feeling lost, so he must regain some direction and influence over his own actions. His war experiences have left him doubting his ability as a soldier and a man. Once he understands the cause of his breakdown, he is even more doubtful as he cannot see why such an 'insignificant' event should have had such a major consequence. Billy's attitude to sex and to Rivers show that he wants to take control, to be in charge where he can, because there are many aspects of his life over which he has no say whatseover.

Prior does not have it all his own way, however. He thinks that he is taking control, but in fact he does allow both Sarah and Rivers to dictate much of what happens to him. When he is granted permanent home service, Billy is disappointed and initially angry with Rivers. However, he soon changes his mind and, in his own way, shows his gratitude to Rivers for helping him. In his relationship with Sarah, he thinks that he has the upper hand most of the time, but it is actually Sarah who sets the pace. He is forced to ask her for sex, rather than forcing it on her, and when he does ask, he seems nervous. Sarah takes charge of the situation, initiating physical contact with him. Later on, when they are alone in Sarah's room, it is Billy who first declares his love. Again he is nervous and unsure of himself - worried perhaps about her response. This is not the self-assured, confidence which Billy would like to believe he exudes.

Most of the men at Craiglockhart are trying to learn to regain control of their lives - that is one of the central points of the novel. These men must come to terms with their experiences and attempt to move on.

MASCULINITY

The style of the novel, its language and opinions are predominantly masculine and, unusually, it appeals to both a male and female audience.

The language used, particularly surrounding Billy Prior, is overtly masculine, occasionally coarse or crude, and this helps us to define his character. It is made clear, by use of language, that he is from a working-class background, without him necessarily saying or doing anything. A different style of writing is used when, for example, Sassoon is the subject. This is meant to demonstrate differences in character and class, as well as attitude.

The characters all exist in a man's world, although many of them feel uncomfortable surrounded by overt masculinity. Although women are present, they are carrying out masculine tasks, and are secondary, but not subservient, characters. The women have adopted male roles - Sarah initiates the conversation with Billy; the factory workers laugh and joke in public in a coarse manner; Sarah has a boyish handshake. All these traits indicate that the adoption of masculine ways has become a necessity for these women, and serve to re-enforce Billy's doubts about his own manhood.

Billy has noticed that women have changed during the war - they have become more masculine - whereas men, and their influence, seem to have diminished. He questions his courage as a result of his breakdown and his need to control his sexual encounters is his way of re-exerting his male authority. However, he is quick and keen to point out to Rivers that he never pays for sex - that would be an easy way out. He prefers to dominate and exert his masculinity over his chosen partner.

Like many officers, Billy has been placed in the role of looking after his men at a young age. Everything from sleeping arrangements, health and emotional problems, to feeding and watering his men have become his responsibility. Rivers recalls this, one evening, realising that many of the men he treats are like mothers to their men - as well as fathers and leaders. He also remembers his personal distaste when a previous patient had referred to him as a male mother, finding this suggestion worrying. He dislikes the implication that a man cannot, of himself, nurture another person - that he must adopt techniques from women, rather than use his own initiative.

In reality, this confusion over the many roles of an officer, caused bewilderment for some officers - one moment they must be a mother-figure, caring and responsible; and the next, they were a soldier, expected to kill and die. Billy Prior does not seem to have particularly enjoyed the 'mothering' aspect of his role in the trenches, possibly finding it demeaning. Sassoon, on the other hand, relished all aspects of his officership and gained the respect of his men, both by his caring attitude to them and the brave example he set in the front line.

HOMOSEXUALITY

It must be borne in mind that during the First World War, any sort of homosexual activity would have been illegal. Not only this, but because of the close proximity of the men, suspicions regarding homosexual behaviour had been aroused. Also, the trial and imprisonment of Oscar Wilde was well within the memory of all concerned. Robert (Robbie) Ross, while being a friend of Sassoon's, had also been involved with Wilde and had many powerful enemies. Sassoon was, therefore, likely to come under the suspicion of the authorities, merely by association.

It is, of course, perfectly possible for one man to love another without there having to be a homosexual nature to their relationship. Owen and Sassoon, for example, were never lovers, but Owen most definitely loved Sassoon in a deeper sense than mere hero-worship. Whether this was a sexual feeling, or it took the form of a more "brotherly" affection and respect is a matter for conjecture.

During the course of *Regeneration*, the main references to homosexuality take place during Sassoon's discussions with Dr Rivers. In reality, during this stage of his life, Sassoon was not a practicing homosexual - he felt a physical attraction to men, especially the young and beautiful - but his sexual orientation was one of confusion more than anything else. Discovery of his sexual ambiguity would have been disastrous for Sassoon, or any other officer for that matter. His discussions on this subject with Rivers in *Regeneration* show the deep trust and respect which existed between these two characters.

The public perception of homosexuality is also reflected within *Regeneration* by the described attitude of Robert Graves who is keen to tell Sassoon of his relationship with Nancy Nicholson. This is done with the sole intention of letting Sassoon know that he is *not* a homosexual himself. The text for this conversation comes from a letter which Graves sent to another poet, and mutual friend of both himself and Sassoon - Robert Nichols. (See *Robert Graves: The Assault Heroic 1895-1926*). One of the effects of his revelation about his sexuality was to leave Sassoon isolated, a feeling which he describes well in *Regeneration*, during a conversation with Rivers. Nichols was a confirmed heterosexual and Graves' denial of any homosexual tendencies led Sassoon to feel that his isolation from two of his closest friends was complete.

During Sassoon's conversations with Rivers, we also learn of the general feeling of distrust, even hatred, of homosexuals felt by politicians, the media and the public. In addition, Graves' assertion that homosexuality can, and should, be 'cured' comes as quite a surprise to Sassoon. His confusion is easy to understand: he is in Craiglockhart to be 'cured' of his anti-war sentiments, and now Graves is implying that he might also need to be 'cured' of his sexual preferences.

THE DEBATE ON FACT IN FICTION

The inclusion of factual content in this, and other, novels relating to the First World War, its necessity and factual accuracy, are topics of great debate amongst historians and academics, as well as students. The opinions of those concerned are varied and, as much as anything, depend upon their own personal viewpoint and taste for these novels themselves. In this section of the study guide, we have outlined some of the factual portrayals - including the less obvious ones - showing their origins. We have also attempted here to portray a fair and balance view of this debate, which we hope will encourage students to trace these sources and, hopefully, form their own perspective on their value in the novel.

Pat Barker has made substantial use of genuine events and characters to add realism to her novel. She has given major roles to real people, including Siegfried Sassoon, Wilfred Owen, Robert Graves and Dr William Rivers. Some of the more minor characters are also genuine personalities, including the doctors at Craiglockhart and many of Sassoon's literary acquaintances and friends. In addition, as well as war-time events and battle references, Pat Barker also alludes to other historical events, such as the controversy surrounding the Pemberton Billing scandal. All of this adds an air of realism, but this should not detract from the fact that this is a story - not a history book, for which it has been known to be mistaken.

The author makes fairly accurate representations of the meetings between Wilfred Owen and Siegfried Sassoon, as well as their treatment while at Craiglockhart and Sassoon's friendship with Dr Rivers. The genuine events are portrayed by Sassoon in two of his prose works: *Siegfried's Journey* (published in 1945), and *The Complete Memoirs of George Sherston* (published in 1937). Neither of these books, in themselves, provides a complete history - in

Siegfried's Journey, Sassoon refers the reader to passages in Sherston's trilogy, in order to save the time of re-writing elements which he had already covered in the earlier work. Even these references, however, are further complicated by the fact that in *The Complete Memoirs of George Sherston*, Sassoon has changed almost all the names of those involved, with the notable exception of Dr Rivers, and Sherston (as Sassoon) is not a poet.

Other events and situations in the novel also have their basis in reality. Among these is the 'eye under the duckboard' scene which Billy Prior recalls while under hypnosis. This event, in almost identical detail, is described in Chapter six of Edmund Blunden's memoir *Undertones of War*. Here Blunden describes the terrible scene of carnage following a direct hit by a shell in the trenches. His sickening description of the remains of a lance-corporal is made even more moving by the arrival on the scene of the dead man's brother, who has to be sent back to headquarters in an almost trance-like state.

In addition to the more obvious sources stated above, Pat Barker also uses more subtle means of reminding the reader about the reality of her subject. These include oblique references to poems, or the topics of poems, which appear occasionally in the text, in addition to the extracts, or whole poems, which are used to great effect to convey Sassoon's state of mind. In chapter one, for example, as Sassoon is boarding the train, he hallucinates about lines of grey men climbing ladders to face the enemy. This line, as it appears in *Regeneration* is taken from his poem *Attack*. Equally, in chapter fourteen, there are two such references within the same paragraph: while in church, studying the stained-glass window, Rivers reflects that men are dying 'not one by one'. This line comes from the poem *Banishment* by Sassoon, which, like *Attack*, was written during his time at Craiglockhart. The second reference in this paragraph is the stained-glass window itself, which depicts the story of Abraham and Isaac. This story is also told in Wilfred Owen's poem *The Parable of the Old Man and the Young*. Rivers thoughts during this brief scene reflect those put forward by Owen in this poem: that the old are slaying the young for the sake of their own pride and self-preservation, while hiding behind religion and the sanctity of the church.

Amongst scholars and historians, there is a debate over whether this mingling of fact and fiction serves a purpose. Some feel that it adds confusion, citing occasions when the book has been treated as historically accurate, providing a true understanding to the reader of the war itself. Some historians and academics seem to find this a worrying concept, finding fault in the concept that a book, which is a story, should be given such historical significance. Others hold the view that any book which can bring the conflict to life and gain the interest of new readers cannot be a bad thing. There is a train of thought that by including realistic people and events, Pat Barker has engaged the average reader in a more proficient way than if she had written a completely fictitious tale. This applies, provided that the reader can separate fact from fiction: a matter which Pat Barker acknowledges and with which she assists in her Author's Note. Readers of pieces like Regeneration must also allow for artistic license - the author's need to amend certain historical or factual content in order to fit in with the plot of the story, or the other characters involved.

One of the main problems in this area arises when the reader forgets to acknowledge these two different elements and assumes that, because of the factual content, *Regeneration* is an entirely accurate narrative, and a sound historical representation of the First World War - something which it does not claim to be.

COMPARISONS

THE EFFECTS OF WAR ON THE INDIVIDUAL

This subject is a popular choice for students making comparisons within this genre. First World War literature is littered with examples of men who have been damaged by their war experiences, and none more so than *Regeneration*. Most of the characters in this novel exhibit symptoms of neurosis - either physical or psychological. Their symptoms depend on the experiences and personality. For example, Burns, who was thrown into the air by an explosion and landed face down in the decomposing stomach of a dead German soldier, is unable to eat and vomits frequently. This physical manifestation of his trauma is allied to an inability to talk about what happened. The case of Burns disturbs Rivers, whose normal method of treatment - forcing a man to face his demons - seems unnecessarily cruel in this instance. He is troubled by how to help Burns, but also by the young man's future which seems bleak.

Not all of the men in Craiglockhart have such an obvious reason for their breakdown. Anderson, for example, having operated on hundreds of mutilated men, suddenly finds himself unable to tolerate the sight of blood. His reactions to seeing blood are extreme and frightening, both for him and those around him. Again, Rivers is troubled by this man's future. He would seem to be finished as a surgeon, but he has a wife and child to support, which makes finding an alternative career imperative. Anderson, on the other hand, would seem to be in denial; believing that he simply needs to rest for a while and then all will be well.

Much of the story in *Regeneration* is told from the perspective of Dr Rivers and his attempts to help his patients come to terms with their experiences. His method of treatment eventually takes its toll and Rivers suffers a nervous breakdown. In this way Pat Barker is demonstrating the power of the imagination - simply by hearing and reliving these horrific experiences, Rivers is also suffering their trauma. It is interesting that the case which seems to haunt Rivers the most is that of Siegfried Sassoon - probably the least 'disturbed' of his patients. Rivers feels responsible for encouraging Sassoon to return to the front: he accepts that from every perspective, he has no alternative, but that does not prevent him feeling guilty when Sassoon finally decides to return. This episode has given Rivers a taste of the officer's role in the trenches: sending men to their deaths and having to live with the consequences.

Another novel which features a psychological reaction to trauma is *The Return of the Soldier* by Rebecca West. This novel was written in 1918 and its author had first-hand experience of life on the home-front during the war. The 'soldier' of the title, Chris Baldry, has been traumatised by some unknown event, or series of events, and has been sent home suffering from amnesia. He is unaware of his marriage, the death of his son, or the war itself and believes that he is still in a relationship with his first love, Margaret. The story centres on the three women in his life: Margaret, his wife Kitty and his cousin Jenny. These women must decide whether to leave Chris in his peaceful safe world with Margaret, or whether to bring him back to reality, his wife Kitty, the reality of his unhappy life and the dangers of war.

Both *Regeneration* and *The Return of the Soldier* pose the question of whether it is always right and justified to 'cure' a person, when to do so may result in greater harm or unhappiness. Rivers continually questions his role in the treatment of his patients, especially that of Sassoon. This is a subject which Rebecca West also addresses in *The Return of the Soldier*. Kitty is the only person who believes that Chris should be 'cured' and her motives are entirely selfish. When her aim is achieved and Chris returns to her, the cost to him is immeasureable. Rebecca West seems to be questioning the role of women in the downfall of men; doubting the necessity to push men further and further until they have nothing left to give. For Pat Barker, the blame seems to lie not with women, but with the authorities, society in general and with the war itself. The scene involving Dr Yealland serves to demonstrate the comparative humanity of Dr Rivers's methods, while brutally forcing the reader to question whether such methods can ever be justified.

Those who have brought about the 'cures' are also sometimes shown to be changed by their experiences. Rivers, right at the end of the novel, admits to himself that his personality has altered. He no longer shies away from conflict, but faces it: his anger at the human cost of the war forces him to question authority in a way he had never imagined possible. Equally, the character of Jenny in *The Return of the Soldier* changes throughout the novel. Initially, like Kitty, she wants Chris to return to normal, she wants to feel his presence in her life again. Gradually, however, she comes to understand that this may not be the best course of action for Chris. She also begins to see Kitty as the selfish, vain woman she really is. The realisation that Chris would be better off with Margaret comes as quite a shock to Jenny, but this is eclipsed by her feelings of regret when she sees his demeanour after he has 'returned' to Kitty: his sorrow is overwhelming.

Another way of showing the effects of the war on the individual is by a more physical manifestation of trauma, although this may not always been genuine. Willard, in *Regeneration*, cannot walk, although there is no medical reason for his paralysis. Willard is concerned that this must mean he is a coward, but Rivers refutes this: it is clear that Willard does not want to return to the front, but a real coward would need the use of his legs in order to run away. This way, Willard can hide from his fear, although Rivers knows that this is not a long-term solution to Willard's problems. His frustration when is wife cannot push him up the hill is seen by Rivers as a minor triumph and he hopes that Willard's exasperation at his own impotence will bring about a speedier recovery. The 'cure' when it happens is less than satisfying for Rivers, as Willard persists in his theory that he had really been paralysed and that Rivers has somehow managed to mend his broken back. Hiding behind a supposed medical problem and living in denial of one's natural fears can also be seen in *Journey's End* by R C Sherriff. Here, Hibbert pretends to been suffering from neuralgia, hoping to be sent back down the line to the Medical Officer. Stanhope is having none of this and refuses to accept that Hibbert is physically ill at all. He confronts Hibbert with this and eventually Hibbert breaks down and confesses that he is terrified of going back into the trenches. Stanhope deals with this situation by admitting his own fears and making Hibbert understand that there is nothing wrong with feeling afraid.

Both authors portray these supposedly 'cowardly' men in an unfavourable light. In the case of Willard, the reader is given the impression that he is quite self-centred. For instance, in the sick-bay, he takes an instant dislike to Billy Prior and asks for him to be moved. His reasons for this are based on his own prejudices and his belief that he is the more 'sick' of the two men. Hibbert is similarly portrayed - given an unfavourable personality which makes it almost impossible to like or sympathise with him. R C Sherriff gives Hibbert many character flaws, making him seem weaker than his fellow officers. This type of portrayal could imply that both authors have a lower opinion of those who tried to escape their duty by pretending to be ill. Equally it could be argued that to stereotype a character in this way is simply a device used to make it easier for the reader to understand the personality of the person involved and saves lengthy explanations of that character's past experiences.

Not all soldiers are seen to be affected by a single traumatic event. Although it was the eye under the duckboard incident which seems to have finally pushed Billy Prior over the edge, it is clear that there has actually been a gradual wearing down of his nerves. Dr Rivers seems to believe that almost any further trauma could have led to Prior's breakdown, no matter how insignificant it might have seemed at the time. He, like Stanhope in *Journey's End*, also reveals something of himself in order to help Prior overcome his doubts: he tells Prior that in the same situation, he would also have broken down.

The character of Stanhope in *Journey's End* seems to have been similarly affected by his length of service and the events which have taken place. Right at the beginning of the play we are told that Stanhope drinks excessively and his behaviour sometimes seems erratic, occasionally bordering on paranoia. These portrayals of men being slowly worn down by the war are realistic and, in both cases, give a sense of clarity to the stories. Everyone will react differently to finding himself in a traumatic situation: the point is that even someone who ordinarily reacts well can be pushed too far.

HEROISM OR HERO-WORSHIP

Heroes come in all different shapes and sizes, and more often than not, their status is dictated either by someone else's or their own perceptions of their actions.

In *Regeneration*, we are reminded several times of the heroism of Siegfried Sassoon. He has won the Military Cross and been recommended for a Victoria Cross; there are tales of his raids into enemy trenches and adventures in No Man's Land. Yet this man has chosen to make a statement against the war and finds himself in the relative security of Craiglockhart. His intention in making the statement, however, had been the publicity of a court-martial, regardless of the personal consequences involved. This requires a different sort of bravery to the conventional, but it is another way of sticking one's head above the parapet. Both Sassoon and the authorities know that to brand him a coward would be impossible, which makes Craiglockhart the only convenient alternative. One could ask whether this course of action required more or less courage than to remain at the front, but in reality, Sassoon did not really see his actions at the front as necessarily heroic, but rather more reckless, based upon anger and frustration.

In the eyes of Wilfred Owen, as portrayed in *Regeneration*, Sassoon's heroic status is undimmed by his Declaration, although this feeling also stems from his respect for Sassoon's poetry and eventually from his growing love for the older man. The reader is forced to question their own perception of a hero: is it someone like Sassoon, who takes great personal risks; or is it someone like Prior, who faces his own perceived failings and desperately wants the chance to prove himself

Some of Sassoon's opinions about heroism can be seen in his poem *The Hero*. One could argue that in this poem, Sassoon is questioning the public perception of heroic behaviour. Why, he seems to ask is

Jack less worthy of remembrance than any other dead soldier? Sassoon's poem was written shortly after he has been awarded his MC and shows that he understood the concepts of fear and desire for self-preservation, but also demonstrates his anger with those who held on to the idea of a 'supreme sacrifice'. Pat Barker echoes this in *Regeneration*, making the reader question whether these 'broken' men are necessarily less worthy than those who have a physical injury.

Returning to the topic of hero-worship, which undoubtedly forms a substantial part of Owen's feelings for Sassoon, this is another common theme of First World War literature. Although Owen's feelings for Sassoon grow through the course of the novel, to the point where his letters start to worry Sassoon, his initial reaction to Sassoon is shown to be one of awe and admiration, despite the fact that he only knows Sassoon by reputation. In *Journey's End*, we can see a different type of hero-worship as Raleigh holds Stanhope in high esteem and has done ever since the were at school together. This makes Raleigh's hero-worship different to Owen's: Sassoon's reputation is based on his war-time heroics and poetry, while Stanhope's is founded on schoolboy encounters. As such this makes Stanhope's position more difficult to maintain, especially as he believes that his hero's crown has slipped. Raleigh's memories of Stanhope are set in a time when, for him to behave 'heroically' was easier: captain of a sport team or head-boy are different positions to leading a company of men in the front line trenches. Like Sassoon, Stanhope has also won an MC which has only served to enhance his heroic status, although due to his own self-doubt, he now finds it almost impossible to live up to Raleigh's expectations.

This element of a fallen hero can also be seen in *Regeneration* as Billy Prior desperately wants to return to the front to prove to himself that he does not lack courage. He believes that by allowing himself to breakdown, he has failed: he takes his neurosis to be a sign of weakness, which can only be refuted by returning to the front.

There are also quieter, more subtle forms of heroism displayed in First World War literature. Rivers, for example, pushes his health - both mental and physical - to the brink in order to help his patients. By listening to their experiences, he also suffers some of their trauma, but is faced with hard decisions and guilt about sending them back to face their fears and, possibly, to die. He doubts his own ability, methods and results, but refuses to believe that the methods of Dr Yealland are more valid or humane than his own. He probably envies Yealland's detachment from his patients.

Other characters exhibit similar traits, such as Osborne in *Journey's End*, who sits quietly before the raid, trying to calm Raleigh's nerves, yet knowing, due to his experience, of the horrors that lie ahead. It could be argued that men like Osborne are probably more heroic because they face their fears, knowing what lies ahead, but still put the needs of others first.

CLASS DIFFERENCES

It is generally acknowledged that the First World War brought about significant changes in the class structure in Britain. Many people found that their pre-war ideas about status and class distinction were now being questioned. Whether the impact of the war was as great as many historians believe is a matter for continuing debate. However, for those living through it, the changes could often be quite obvious and frequently caused great confusion.

There is a definite class difference portrayed in *Regeneration*. All of the men at Craiglockhart are officers, and most seem to come from the upper classes. We are told, for example, that Anderson needs to give some thought to his future career as he will soon have to consider paying school fees; equally Burns's parents are kept busy in London, but also maintain a house on the Suffolk coast. The exception to this rule is Billy Prior, who comes from a working-class northern background. This is clear from the appearance and behaviour of his parents, as well as his own attitude and demeanour, but Pat Barker reinforces this by the language she uses when Billy Prior is involved in the story.

Prior's character seems to have a chip on his shoulder about his treatment by the upper-class officers. He derides them and their opinions, seeking always to distance himself from association with them. We do not, for example, hear of his socialising with any of his fellow officers, as he prefers to leave Craiglockhart and seek solace among people whose company he finds more acceptable. This sense of feeling out of place was common during the war amongst those who were perceived to be from a socially inferior background. Like Billy, they sensed that they did not belong with the men any more than they did with the officers. Such men were called "Temporary Gentlemen" which in itself shows the snobbery which was attached to this kind of officer.

Rivers points out other differences between the men and the officers, which only serves to further confuse Prior. He displays the same symptoms as a ranking soldier, but receives the medical treatment of an officer. Billy Prior's strong sense of injustice would probably make him resent the fact that an ordinary soldier would not receive the same allowances as he has.

The character of Trotter in R C Sherriff's *Journey's End* is in a similar predicament. Trotter has risen from the ranks, but the audience is never actually told what his upbringing was. Instead Sherriff has Trotter use more colloquial language than the other officers in the dugout to demonstrate the differences in their status. Trotter is much more reticent of discuss his feelings with the others, which leads Stanhope to suggest jealously that Trotter *has* no feelings. However, for Trotter, like Billy Prior, the sense of not really belonging makes it much more difficult for him to be open with his comrades as he knows that his wartime equality is only temporary.

The portrayal of both of these characters underlines the fact that, for someone at that time to rise above his 'station' in life was a daunting and often impossible task. While the class structure was beginning to change, this was a slow process. After the war, the wealthy would no longer have large households of staff, but they would still be wealthy; the poor would eventually gain better housing and a welfare state, but by comparison, they would still be poor.

A QUESTION OF COMPARISONS

Many students have to make direct comparisons between two particular texts, demonstrating the author's treatment of a specific topic. Where this is dealt with as coursework, some examination boards allow that the student may be permitted to choose the texts for themselves. To that end, we have included a list of possible topics and suggested texts which, in our opinion, provide suitable material for such essays, assuming that *Regeneration* will be one of the texts involved. The notes provided, together with the more detailed information in the previous chapter, are intended to whet the appetite, rather than provide the 'answers'. Whenever a student chooses to use *Regeneration* as part of a piece of comparative work, they should allow for the fact that much of Pat Barker's novel is based in fact, but also that it is still a novel - not a piece of history.

THE ROLE OF WOMEN

War, being at that time essentially a male domain, means that in the literature of the First World War, the role of women can often be minimalised. Students could choose to look at how authors represent women, focusing possibly on their changing role in society, or their reactions to the war itself.

Using Regeneration and The Return of the Soldier

The Return of the Soldier focuses on the predicament of three women who must decide whether to leave the soldier, Chris Baldry, in his safe world, where he believes himself to be 21 years old and still in love with down-to-earth, working-class Margaret, or return him to normal - a 36 year old soldier, who is married to beautiful but selfish Kitty. The effects of his amnesia have far-reaching consequences, but the decision about his future, ultimately lies with these women. Rebecca West, the author of this novel, chooses to tell the story though the eyes of Chris's cousin, Jenny, who has always loved Chris, thus giving the story an even more complicated bias. Jenny believes that she has Chris's best interests at heart, but over the course of the novel, she begins to question her own motives and opinions. The three women in this novel are all very different: Kitty is self-centred and arrogant; Margaret is shy but determined to do the best for Chris; Jenny, however, has effectively sacrificed her own happiness just to be with Chris. She now doubts whether this was the best thing she could have done.

The representation of these three women is very different from the women in *Regeneration*. This is partly because of their class - although Margaret, in *The Return of the Soldier*, is working-class. But also because of where they live, the work they do and the impact which the war has had on their own relationships and lifestyles. The women in *Regeneration* are independent, self-assured and, to a certain extent, have fairly masculine outlooks.

Rebecca West's treatment of women in the war is very different from Pat Barker's. Women play an important part in *The Return of the Soldier* - in fact the whole plot is based around them. In *Regeneration*, the women seem less important and their roles are less varied, but their impact - particularly that of Sarah - is vital to the reader's understanding of the characters and the effects of the war on society.

THE EFFECTS OF THE WAR ON RELATIONSHIPS

Students who choose to study this topic could look at either relationships which existed before the war, paying attention to the impact of the conflict; or those which have been formed during the course of the war. Equally, students could focus on exclusively male relationships, or those between men and women or children and parents.

Using Regeneration and Strange Meeting

Strange Meeting follows the close relationship between David Barton and John Hilliard, who meet in France during 1916. Their friendship soon turns to love, although the author does not make it clear whether theirs is a physical relationship. Students could choose to compare Susan Hill's treatment of this relationship with Pat Barker's portrayal of the growing friendship between Wilfred Owen and Siegfried Sassoon in *Regeneration*.

Barton and Hilliard, for example, openly confess their love for one another, despite the dangerous consequences of their feelings. This is a freedom which is not afforded to Sassoon and Owen: Sassoon is already in a vulnerable position as far as the authorities are concerned, and Owen is simply too shy to declare his feelings in this way, although his subsequent letters certainly seem to make Sassoon wary. Pat Barker, in including real people in her novel, naturally has to adhere to reality in this instance. Susan Hill, however, allows her characters to effectively throw caution to the wind. She makes it very clear that the most important aspect of her novel is love itself.

In both instances, these relationships have been formed during the course of the war, without which they may not have occurred in the first place. The impact of the war, it could be argued, has been to allow the friendships to begin in the first place. Sassoon seems to be less affected by their relationship than Owen, whose sense of loss when he leaves Sassoon is too great to be measured. For Hilliard, although Barton dies, his life has been so deeply affected, that he knows it will never be the same again - not because of the war, however, but because of love.

HEALING

This topic could encompass the physical or emotional healing of a man who has been damaged by the war; or it could include the theme of forgiveness, or learning to live with the past.

Using Regeneration and Birdsong

Birdsong by Sebastian Faulks tells the story of Stephen Wraysford, a young man whose unsuccessful pre-war love affair has damaged him emotionally. His wartime experiences initially do not appear to affect him, because he has buried his emotions deep within himself. However, as the novel progresses, the reader comes to understand the effect of the war, and love, on this man.

Like Billy Prior, Stephen Wraysford has has a difficult childhood. He has accepted this, however, and it is his love affair with Isabelle Azaire, four years before the war, which really seems to shape his personality. It is not really until Stephen is buried underground that he discovers a will to live: to survive and face the future.

Billy's needs are different: he needs to go back to France, to prove to himself that he is courageous. First, however, he must learn to accept what has happened to him and learn from it. Given his personality, this is something which he is reluctant to accept - believing that men like him don't suffer from breakdowns.

It is this growing acceptance of one's situation and learning to deal with the past which forms one of the themes for both of these novels. Both Pat Barker and Sebastian Faulks present their readers with flawed heroes - both of them have character traits which makes it difficult to always like them. However, both the other characters in the novels, and the readers themselves come to like these men.

FURTHER READING RECOMMENDATIONS FOR A-LEVEL STUDENTS

Students of A-Level standard are expected to demonstrate a sound knowledge of the texts they are studying and also to enhance this knowledge with extensive reading of other texts within the subject. We have provided on the following pages a list of books, poetry, plays and non-fiction which, in our opinion, provide a good basic understanding of this topic.

Plays and Drama

Journey's End by R C Sherriff
A play, written from first-hand experience, which describes three days in the lives of five officers and their servant during the build-up to the German spring offensive in March 1918. Set in a dug-out in the trenches near St Quentin, this moving play has become a standard text for GCSE and A-Level students.

The Accrington Pals by Peter Whelan
This play follows a group of men who have volunteered to join their local Pals battalion. Written from the perspective of those who are left behind, we are shown the impact on their everyday lives when almost all of the men have gone away to fight. The realistic tragedy of this play is that when the Pals participated in the Battle of the Somme towns, such as Accrington, suffered great losses which would affect almost every inhabitant.

Oh! What a Lovely War by Joan Littlewood
A satire about the First World War told using newsreels, documents and songs. First performed in 1963, this is as much a play about the 1960's as about the First World War and promotes the 'Lions led by Donkeys' theory which was prevalent at that time.

Not About Heroes by Stephen MacDonald
Probably one of the most underrated First World War plays, this details the friendship between Wilfred Owen and Siegfried Sassoon, from their initial meeting at Craiglockhart, to Owen's death. Told from Sassoon's perspective, it is a humourous, tragic and above all, moving account of this friendship and is based on diary entries and extracts from letters and autobiographies.

In addition, students of could also watch *Blackadder Goes Forth* starring Rowan Atkinson paying particular attention to the final episode. Although this screenplay was written in the late 20th century, much of the atmosphere and 'gallows' humour could prove useful in understanding this play, especially when students are unable to see a live performance.

Novels

Strange Meeting by Susan Hill
Strange Meeting is a beautiful and moving book. It is the story of two young men, who meet in the worst circumstances, yet manage to overcome their surroundings and form a deep and lasting friendship. Susan Hill writes so evocatively that the reader is automatically drawn into the lives of these men: the sights, sounds and even smells which they witness are brought to life. It is a book about war and its effects; it is also a story of love, both conventional and 'forbidden'; of human relationships of every variety. This is a tale told during the worst of times, about the best of men.

Birdsong by Sebastian Faulks
This novel tells the story of Stephen Wraysford, his destructive pre-war love-affair, his war experiences and, through the eyes of his grand-daughter, the effects of the war on his personality and his generation. A central theme to this story is man's ability to

overcome adversity: to rise above his circumstances and survive - no matter what is thrown in his path.

A Long Long Way by Sebastian Barry
This is a story about Willie Dunne, a young Irish volunteer serving in the trenches of the Western Front. Willie must not only contend with the horrors of the war, but also his own confused feelings regarding the Easter uprising of 1916, and his father's disapproval. This novel is about loyalty, betrayal, fear, wisdom, discovery and, above all, love.

A Very Long Engagement by Sebastien Japrisot
This is a story of enduring love and determination. Refusing to believe that her lover can possibly have left her forever, Mathilde decides to search for Manech whom she has been told is missing, presumed dead. She learns from a first-hand witness, that he may not have died, so she sets out on a voyage of discovery - learning not just about his fate, but also a great deal about herself and human nature.

The Return of the Soldier by Rebecca West
Written in 1918, this home-front novel gives a useful insight into the trauma of war, as seen through the eyes of three women. Chris Baldry, an officer and husband of Kitty, returns home suffering from shell-shock and amnesia, believing that he is still in a relationship with Margaret Allington - his first love. Kitty, Margaret and Chris's cousin, Jenny, must decide whether to leave Chris in his make-believe world, safe from the war; or whether to 'cure' him and risk his future welfare once he returns to being a soldier.

All Quiet on the Western Front by Erich Maria Remarque
Written from first-hand experience of life in the trenches, this novel is the moving account of the lives of a group of young German soldiers during the First World War. The fact that this, often shocking, story is told from a German perspective demonstrates

the universal horrors of the war and the sympathy between men of both sides for others enduring the same hardships as themselves.

Poetry

It is recommended that students read from a wide variety of poets, including female writers. The following anthologies provide good resources for students.

Poems of the First World War - Never such Innocence
Edited by Martin Stephen
Probably one of the most comprehensive and accessible anthologies of First World War poetry. The notes which accompany each chapter are not over-long or too complicated and leave the poetry to speak for itself.

Lads: Love Poetry of the Trenches by Martin Taylor
Featuring many lesser-known poets and poems, this anthology approaches the First World War from a different perspective: love. A valuable introduction discusses the emotions of men who, perhaps for the first time, were discovering their own capacity to love their fellow man. This is not an anthology of purely homo-erotic poems, but also features verses by those who had found affection and deep lasting friendship in the trenches of the First World War.

Scars Upon My Heart, Selected by Catherine Reilly
A collection of poems written exclusively by women on the subject of the First World War. Some of the better known female poets are featured here, together with the more obscure, and authors who are not now renowned for their poetry, but for their works in other areas of literature.

Non-Fiction

Undertones of War by Edmund Blunden
Edmund Blunden's memoir of his experiences in the First World
War is a moving and enlightening book, demonstrating above all the
intense feelings of respect and comradeship which Blunden found in
the trenches.

The Complete Memoirs of George Sherston by Siegfried Sassoon
This book is an autobiographical, fictionalised account of Sassoon's
life during the First World War. Sassoon has changed the names of
the characters and George Sherston (Sassoon) is not a poet.
Sassoon became one of the war's most famous poets and this prose
account of his war provides useful background information.
(For a list of the fictional characters and their factual counterparts,
see Appendix II of *Siegfried Sassoon by John Stuart Roberts*.)

The Western Front by Richard Holmes
This is one of many history books about the First World War.
Dealing specifically with the Western Front, Richard Holmes looks
at the creation of the trench warfare system, supplying men and
munitions, major battles and living on the front line.

*Letters from a Lost Generation (First World War Letters of Vera Brittain
and Four Friends)*
Edited by Alan Bishop and Mark Bostridge
A remarkable insight into the changes which the First World War
caused to a particular set of individuals. In this instance, Vera Brittain
lost four important people in her life (two close friends, her fiancé
and her brother). The agony this evoked is demonstrated through
letters sent between these five characters, which went on to form
the basis of Vera Brittain's autobiography *Testament of Youth*.

1914-1918: Voices and Images of the Great War by Lyn MacDonald
One of the most useful 'unofficial' history books available to those
studying the First World War. As with all of Lyn MacDonald's
excellent works, this book tells the story of the soldiers who fought
the war through their letters, diary extracts, newspaper reports,
poetry and eye-witness accounts. The author gives just the right
amount of background information of a political and historical
nature to keep the reader interested and informed, while leaving
the centre-stage to those who really matter... the men themselves.

GENERAL ADVICE TO STUDENTS

Although examinations can seem daunting, especially when the topic is as wide as First World War Literature, it is worth remembering the following simple tips:

- Be prepared. Read as much as possible beforehand; make sure you have revised well enough.

- Read the question. In other words, read it carefully, several times if necessary to be sure that you have a full understanding of what is expected. It is a very simple mistake to think you have understood the requirements only to find that you have completely misinterpreted them.

- Answer the question. Another common error is to get stuck in a train of thought and forget that what you are writing might not actually be answering the question in hand. You should stick to the topic required, even though you might have thought of a brilliant piece of analysis - if it doesn't relate to the question, it doesn't belong in your essay.

- Allow enough time. The examination paper will give you a guide as to how long to allow for each question. Think about the fact that you must plan your essay, deciding in advance how you want to approach the topic in hand. Don't forget to allow a few minutes at the end, just to check over what you have written.

Good luck!

BIBLIOGRAPHY

Lads
by Martin Taylor

Minds at War – The Poetry and Experience of the First World War
Edited by David Roberts

Siegfried Sassoon - the War Poems
Edited by Rupert Hart-Davis

The First World War
by John Keegan

Siegfried Sassoon - A Biography
by Max Egremont

Siegfried Sassoon - The Making of A War Poet - a Biography
by Jean Moorcroft Wilson

Siegfried Sassoon
by John Stuart Roberts

Wilfred Owen - War Poems and Others
Edited by Dominic Hibberd

Anthem for Doomed Youth
by Jon Stallworthy

Violets from Oversea
by Tonie and Valmai Holt

Siegfried's Journey
by Siegfried Sassoon

Undertones of War
by Edmund Blunden

British Culture and the First World War
by George Robb

The Cambridge Companion to the Literature of The First World War
Edited by Vincent Sherry

OTHER GREAT WAR LITERATURE
STUDY GUIDE TITLES

Great War Literature Study Guide Paperbacks:

Title	ISBN
All Quiet on the Western Front	978-1905378302
Birdsong	978-1905378234
Journey's End - GCSE	978-1905378371
Journey's End - A-Level	978-1905378401
Strange Meeting	978-1905378210
The Return of the Soldier	978-1905378357
Female Poets of the First World War - Vol.1	978-1905378258
War Poets of the First World War - Vol.1	978-1905378241

Great War Literature Study Guide E-Books:

Novels & Plays
All Quiet on the Western Front
Birdsong
Journey's End
Regeneration
Strange Meeting
The Return of the Soldier

Poets
Harold Begbie
Rupert Brooke
Female War Poets 1: WM Letts; M Postgate Cole; E Nesbit
Female War Poets 2: MW Cannan; K Tynan; C Mew
Female War Poets 3: N Cunard; I Tree; E Farjeon
Wilfrid Wilson Gibson

Julian Grenfell

Ivor Gurney

E A Mackintosh

John McCrae

Robert Nichols

Wilfred Owen

Jessie Pope

Isaac Rosenberg

Siegfried Sassoon

Charles Hamilton Sorley

Edward Thomas

Robert Ernest Vernède

Arthur Graeme West

Please note that e-books are only available direct from our Web site at www.greatwarliterature.co.uk and cannot be purchased through bookshops.